AF270602

ATLANTA FALCONS

KENNY ABDO

Fly!
An Imprint of Abdo Zoom
abdobooks.com

abdobooks.com

Published by Abdo Zoom, a division of ABDO, P.O. Box 398166, Minneapolis, Minnesota 55439. Copyright © 2022 by Abdo Consulting Group, Inc. International copyrights reserved in all countries. No part of this book may be reproduced in any form without written permission from the publisher. Fly!™ is a trademark and logo of Abdo Zoom.

Printed in China.
052021
092021

Photo Credits: AP Images, Icon Sportswire, iStock, Newscom, Shutterstock PREMIER
Production Contributors: Kenny Abdo, Jennie Forsberg, Grace Hansen
Design Contributors: Candice Keimig, Neil Klinepier

Library of Congress Control Number: 2020919474

Publisher's Cataloging-in-Publication Data

Names: Abdo, Kenny, author.
Title: Atlanta Falcons / by Kenny Abdo
Description: Minneapolis, Minnesota : Abdo Zoom, 2022 | Series: NFL teams |
    Includes online resources and index.
Identifiers: ISBN 9781098224523 (lib. bdg.) | ISBN 9781098225469 (ebook) |
    ISBN 9781098225933 (Read-to-Me ebook)
Subjects: LCSH: Atlanta Falcons (Football team)--Juvenile literature. | National Football
    League--Juvenile literature. | Football teams--Juvenile literature. | American
    football--Juvenile literature. | Professional sports--Juvenile literature.
Classification: DDC 796.33264--dc23

TABLE OF CONTENTS

ATLANTA FALCONS

Playing more than 55 years in the NFL brings its highs and lows, but the Atlanta Falcons have always soared on.

From playoff wins to dancing the Dirty Bird, the Falcons are a team that truly rises up.

The Falcons were founded in 1965 by Rankin M. Smith Sr. They became the fifteenth team to join the NFL.

The team first played in 1966 but struggled. The Falcons didn't have a winning season until 1971.

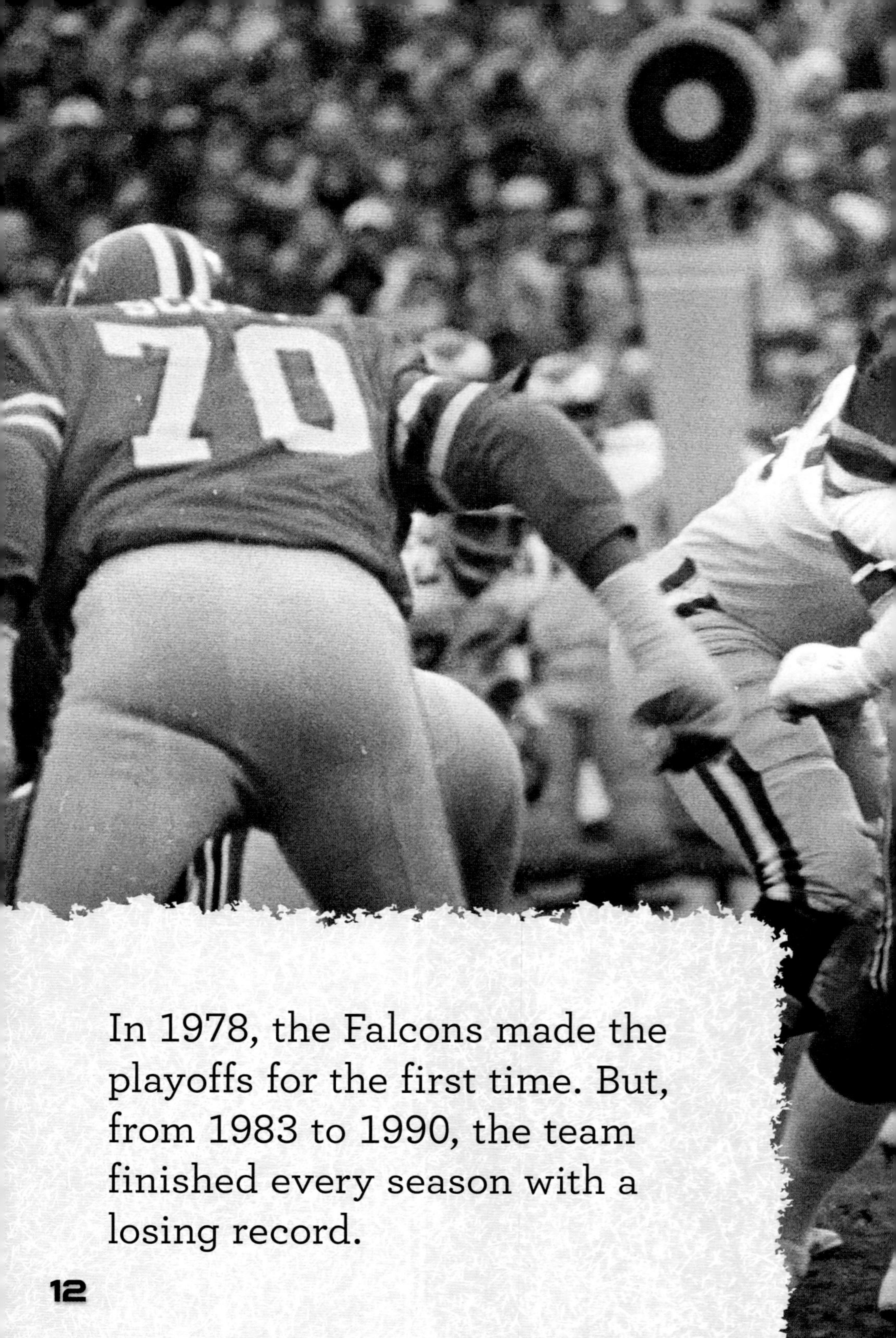

In 1978, the Falcons made the playoffs for the first time. But, from 1983 to 1990, the team finished every season with a losing record.

TEAM RECAPS

In 1998, the Falcons won their division with a team record of 14 wins. In the playoffs, they beat the San Francisco 49ers and the Minnesota Vikings. Then they played in their first **Super Bowl** but they lost to the Denver Broncos.

The Falcons made it to the 2002 playoffs. They beat the Green Bay Packers in a **Wild Card** game at Lambeau Field. No other team had done that before. The Falcons had made NFL history!

The Falcons won 11 games and made it to the **NFC championship** in the 2004 season. In 2012, the team again made it to the NFC championship. But they lost to the San Francisco 49ers.

In 2017, the Falcons went to **Super Bowl** LI! They led the game in points for the first half. However, the Falcons lost in overtime to the New England Patriots 34-28.

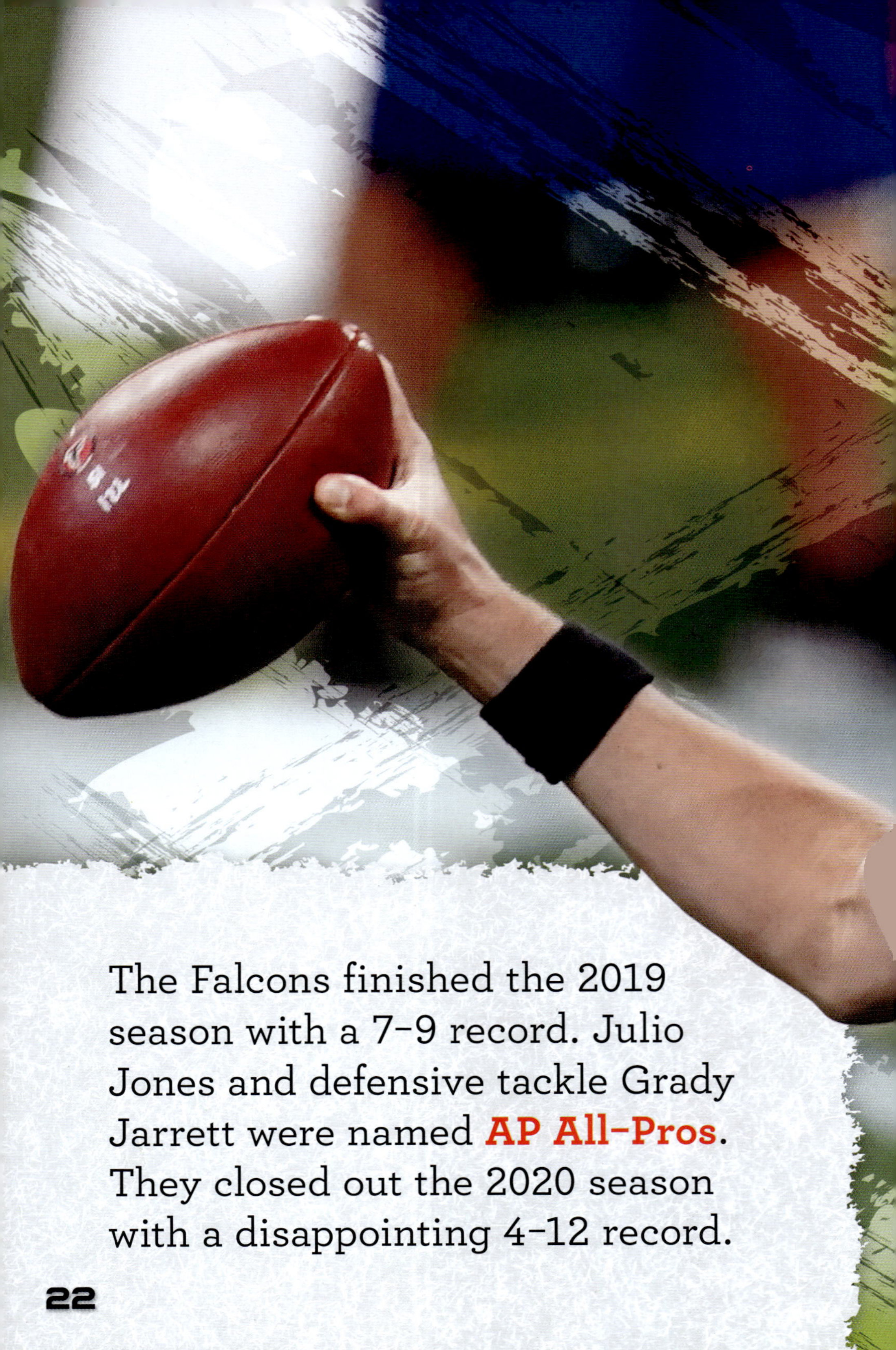

The Falcons finished the 2019 season with a 7-9 record. Julio Jones and defensive tackle Grady Jarrett were named **AP All-Pros**. They closed out the 2020 season with a disappointing 4-12 record.

HALL OF FAME

Steve Bartkowski was the first pick in the 1975 **draft**. He was named NFL **Rookie** of the Year after throwing for more than 1,600 yards. Bartkowski set every team passing record. He threw an amazing 154 touchdown passes in 123 games!

Deion Sanders was an athlete who earned his nickname, "Prime Time." He had ten touchdowns and 24 **interceptions** during his short Falcons career. Sanders was **inducted** into the Pro Football Hall of Fame in 2011.

Matt Ryan threw for 3,440 yards in his first year with the Falcons. He won the NFL Offensive **Rookie** of the Year Award. From 2008 to 2020, Ryan completed more than 55,000 yards, putting him in the top 10 of passing leaders in NFL history!

GLOSSARY

AP All-Pro – an honor given by press organizations to professional NFL players that names the best player at each position during a season.

championship – a game held to find a first-place winner.

draft – a process in sports to assign athletes to a certain team.

induct – to admit someone as a member of an organization.

interception – when a player catches a pass that was meant for the other team's player.

National Football Conference (NFC) – one of two major conferences of the NFL. Each conference contains 16 teams split into four divisions. The winner of the NFC championship plays the AFC.

rookie – a first-year player in a professional sport.

Super Bowl – the NFL championship game, played once a year.

Wild Card Round – the first round of the playoffs. Each of the two conferences send four division champions and three wild-card teams to its postseason.

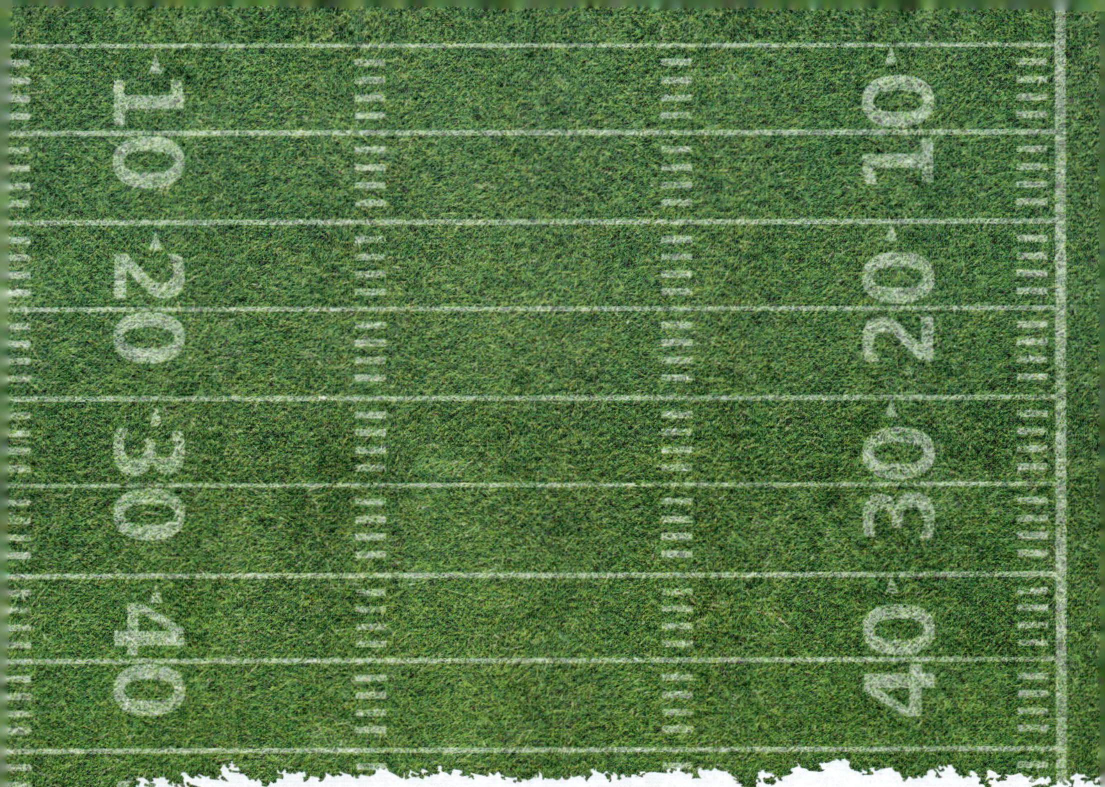

ONLINE RESOURCES

To learn more about the Atlanta Falcons, please visit **abdobooklinks.com** or scan this QR code. These links are routinely monitored and updated to provide the most current information available.